YOUR KNOWLEDGE HAS

Claudius Benedikt Hildebrand

Impact of the UMTS Experience for Forthcoming Network Generations

GRIN Verlag

Bibliografische Information der Deutschen Nationalbibliothek:

Die Deutsche Bibliothek verzeichnet diese Publikation in der Deutschen National-
bibliografie; detaillierte bibliografische Daten sind im Internet über http://dnb.d-
nb.de/ abrufbar.

Dieses Werk sowie alle darin enthaltenen einzelnen Beiträge und Abbildungen
sind urheberrechtlich geschützt. Jede Verwertung, die nicht ausdrücklich vom
Urheberrechtsschutz zugelassen ist, bedarf der vorherigen Zustimmung des Verla-
ges. Das gilt insbesondere für Vervielfältigungen, Bearbeitungen, Übersetzungen,
Mikroverfilmungen, Auswertungen durch Datenbanken und für die Einspeicherung
und Verarbeitung in elektronische Systeme. Alle Rechte, auch die des auszugsweisen
Nachdrucks, der fotomechanischen Wiedergabe (einschließlich Mikrokopie) sowie
der Auswertung durch Datenbanken oder ähnliche Einrichtungen, vorbehalten.

Imprint:

Copyright © 2003 GRIN Verlag GmbH
Druck und Bindung: Books on Demand GmbH, Norderstedt Germany
ISBN: 978-3-638-64625-3

This book at GRIN:

http://www.grin.com/en/e-book/19701/impact-of-the-umts-experience-for-forthco-
ming-network-generations

GRIN - Your knowledge has value

Der GRIN Verlag publiziert seit 1998 wissenschaftliche Arbeiten von Studenten, Hochschullehrern und anderen Akademikern als eBook und gedrucktes Buch. Die Verlagswebsite www.grin.com ist die ideale Plattform zur Veröffentlichung von Hausarbeiten, Abschlussarbeiten, wissenschaftlichen Aufsätzen, Dissertationen und Fachbüchern.

Visit us on the internet:

http://www.grin.com/

http://www.facebook.com/grincom

http://www.twitter.com/grin_com

EUROPEAN BUSINESS SCHOOL

University Schloss Reichartshausen

Seminar Paper

within the scope of the seminar in Information Systems

Winter Semester 2003

Impact of the UMTS Experience for Forthcoming Network Generations

Name: Claudius Benedikt Hildebrand

Due Date: 10. October 2003

Table of Contents

Abbreviations

1G	First Generation
2G	Second Generation
3G	Third Generation
4G	Fourth Generation
5G	Fifth Generation
ANSI	American National Standardization Institute
ATM	Asynchronous Transfer Mode
bps	Bits per Second
CDMA	Code Division Multiple Access
CDMA2000	Code Division Multiple Access – Revision 2000
cdmaOne	Code Division Multiple Access – Revision 1 (ANSI 41 / IS-95)
DCS	Digital Cellular System
EDGE	Enhanced Data rates for Global Evolution
FDD	Frequency Division Duplex
FDMA	Frequency Division Multiple Access
GPRS	General Packet Radio Service
GSM	Global System for Mobile Communication (formerly: Groupe Speciale Mobile)
HSCSD	High Speed Circuit Switched Data
HSDPA	High Speed Downlink Packet Access
IMT-2000	International Mobile Telecommunications at 2000 MHz
IP	Internet Protocol
ISDN	Integrated Services Digital Network
ITU	International Telecommunication Union
kbps	Kilobits per Second
Mbps	Megabits per Second
MHz	Mega Hertz
MMS	Multimedia Message Service
PDA	Personal Digital Assistant
PDC	Personal Digital Cellular
SIM	Subscriber Identity Module
SMS	Short Message Service

TD-CDMA	Time Division – Code Division Multiple Access
TDD	Time Division Duplex
TDMA	Time Division Multiple Access
UMTS	Universal Mobile Telecommunication System
UWC	Universal Wireless Consortium
VSF-CDMA	Variable Spreading Factor Code Division Multiple Access
VSF-OFCDM	Variable Spreading Factor Orthogonal Frequency and Code Division Multiplexing
WAP	Wireless Application Protocol
W-CDMA	Wideband Code Division Multiple Access
WLAN	Wireless Local Area Network

1. Introduction

1.1. Problem Definition and Goals of the Study

In the year 2000 when billions of Euro were spent for licenses to be used in Third Generation (=3G) mobile phone networks, operators promised customers a large variety of new services and high speeds for mobile internet access in short future. Now, three years later, the big picture looks different. Even though the number of subscribers to mobile services increased to 1.3 billion users worldwide using primarily Second Generation (=2G) networks (Cellular Online, 2003), there seems to be customer skepticism towards 3G due to several reasons that are going to be analyzed in this paper. Mobile operators estimated a huge demand in data services and consequently spend lots of money trying to provide these services, but customer demand lags behind. (Slodczyk, 2003) This might not only affect the launch of 3G, but also impact upcoming Fourth Generation (=4G) networks. 4G is "often referred as 'digital convergence' (Koljonen, 2001, p. 1) which means that it will be able to offer a unified communication platform for a large number of devices in heterogeneous environments at high speeds. 3G which is marketed as Universal Mobile Telecommunications System (=UMTS) in Europe, was regarded as a first step towards delivering multimedia content using a universal standard around the world. However, current development shows some stumbling blocks that might negatively impact the acceptance of UMTS. This paper will analyze the evaluation of mobile services from the beginning on with a special focus on 3G and 4G.

1.2. Outline

This paper evaluates the impact of the UMTS experience for forthcoming network generations. Therefore, it is necessary to show the development of mobile networks from the beginning on. During the evolution process, formerly analogue networks transformed to digital ones with more and more services that added value to customers' life and consequently became very popular. In these days, mobile operators are trying to migrate their second generation networks to third generation which was supposed to be a globally accepted standard offering high data transfer speeds. However, an in-depth look at the technical and financial background of the 3G implementation shows that provider promises and user expectations differ. This will not only affect 3G, but also upcoming network generations like 4G. In the following, continuous delays in the 3G launch and advanced research in 4G technology in combination with upgrades to existing 2G network infrastructure are discovered as threads questioning the success of 3G.

2. The Evolution Path to 3G Cellular Networks from a Historical Perspective

2.1. First Generation – The Stone Age of Mobile Communications

The first generation of mobile networks (=1G) were established in the 1950s. These networks were not connected to a country-wide backbone network, but only covered a limited geographical area of one cell site. Roaming, which means using a mobile hand-held device in another network, was not possible in these days. Moreover, these isolated applications were not connected to each other and a human operator was required to manually establish connections between the caller and callee. This proved to be very costly and unsatisfying. Therefore, telecommunication companies started to connect those islands of mobile coverage. In Germany for example, the so-called "A-Netz" (1958 – 1977) was the first analogue mobile network which covered 80% of the German territory when it had been established. The "B-Netz" (1972 – 1994) was the next step in the development and allowed self-dialing which made operators redundant. In 1986, the "C-Netz" was launched which used first simple multiplexing techniques for more efficient frequency use and allowed data transmissions via modem of up to 2400 bits per second (=bps). In 1992, almost area-wide network coverage was achieved by using about 1900 transmitters. End of 2000, the "C-Netz" was finally switched off. (Schreiber, 2002, p. 36-40)

2.2. Second Generation – Entering the Mediaeval Times of Digital Mobile Communication

First Generation mobile networks offered a very valuable service in these days when they were set up but customer demands and ongoing globalization urged mobile service providers to offer new services and to cope with future growth. To achieve this, it was necessary to replace analogue transmission techniques that were used in 1G networks by digital ones which did not only offer higher voice quality, but also more efficient frequency use, compatibility with landline communication systems, error correcting, interference resistance and lower costs for installation and use. (Walke, 2001, p. 135-139) In 1982, major European telecommunication companies decided to develop a pan-European cellular network. The so-called working group 'Groupe Speciale Mobile' was established which set the standards for this network. In 1991, the first Second Generation digital networks were set up in several European countries using a frequency of 900 Megahertz (=MHz). Telekom D1 (today: T-Mobile) and Mannesmann D2 (today: Vodafone) are two examples of 2G networks that were launched 1992 in Germany. However, the development of the Global System for Mobile Communication (=GSM) standard continued. This led to the definition of the Digital Cellular System (=DCS) 1800 standard which was used by E-Plus and Viag Interkom (today: O2) to provide services similar to GSM 900 but using a frequency of 1800 MHz. (Duque-Antón, 2002, p. 63-64) To use the limited frequency band efficiently, a combination of the multiplexing techniques Time Division Multiple Access (= TDMA – using a very short time slot only on a certain frequency) and Frequency Division Multiple Access (=FDMA – using only a small band of the available frequency) was used.[1] European mobile phone users were now able to use their devices not only in their home country, but also in other European or international countries which used the GSM/DCS technology. However, it was necessary to have a mobile phone that was capable of using the 900 MHz or the 1800 MHz band. Only so-called Dual-Band phones were able to use both network types with either of these European standards.

But there was also unattached research in 2G both in the USA and in Japan. Consequently, different 2G systems were installed in these countries which were not compatible with the European GSM standard. Even though some of them used similar multiplexing techniques, the network infrastructure and frequencies are different. So it is not possible to use these handsets in other network environments. In the USA, the Code Division Multiple Access Revision One (=cdmaOne) standard is used which is specified in IS-95 using software codes to extend bandwidth whereas in Japanese Personal Digital Cellular (=PDC) only used TDMA in their mobile networks. Due to different identification processes (e.g. SIM-Card for GSM phones), it was not possible to built devices that could be used in all these different network environments. (Lescuyer, 2002, p. 1-49)

2G networks were designed primarily for voice communication. The internet boom in the late 1990s and new multimedia applications created a demand for more bandwidth for data communication not only on landline connections, but also for mobile devices. This could not be handled with the initial 2G definitions that only allowed a bandwidth of 9600 bps in GSM systems. Therefore, new 'phases' of GSM were developed which did not only offer more bandwidth using techniques like General Packet Radio Service (=GPRS) or High Speed Circuit Switched Data (=HSCSD), but also new services like Wireless Application Protocol (=WAP) for mobile internet access, Short Message Service (=SMS) or Multimedia Message Service (=MMS). The first and second 'phase' of

[1] Further reading about Multiplexing Techniques: Walke, B. (2001). Mobilfunknetze *und ihre Protokolle 1 – Grundlagen, GSM, UMTS und andere zellulare Mobilfunknetze* (3rd ed.). Stuttgart: Teubner.

GSM (1991/1994) mostly covered connection-oriented services whereas phase 2+ also defines connection-less (packet-based) services and transmission technologies which can be regarded as another step forwards the next generation in the evolution of mobile communications. (Duque-Antón, 2002, p. 63-74)

Amongst the competing 2G technologies, GSM is the most popular one with about 880 million users worldwide in August 2003 whereas only 164 million people subscribed to Code Division Multiple Access (=CDMA) based networks and another 120 million people used TDMA-based technologies for mobile communications. GSM was intended to be a European-wide standard but it was that successful so nowadays it is used in 187 countries worldwide (Cellular Online, 2003).

3. Third Generation – Stepping into a new Generation of Mobile Communications

3.1. User Expectations and Mobile Service Provider Promises of 3G Systems

2G mobile systems have proved to be a real success and gained wide acceptance amongst people both in developed and in developing countries. Declining prices and a large variety of services, especially the so-called killer-application SMS contributed to the success of mobile phones and raised expectations of future generations and services.

Data services are supposed to be the new cash-cows of mobile service providers in the next decade. According to research by the UMTS-Forum (2002, p. 3), data or non-voice services will account for 50% of mobile operator's revenues in 2005/6 in comparison to 2001 where 90% of their revenue was generated by voice services. The number of SMS sent per user rocketed and made SMS to the so-called killer-application in 2G systems with 366 billion messages sent in the year 2002 worldwide (Cellular Online, 2003).

This leads to the question of which types of services users expect in 3G systems and what the future cash-cows of mobile service providers will be.

Being asked about the most important service consumers would like to use with 3G is surprisingly still SMS. SMS were mentioned by 81% of all people asked followed by local news like weather or traffic that were useful to 71% of them. About 70% of all surveyed people are looking forward to use their 3G cellphone for picture messaging and video conferencing followed by messaging and news. Watching TV or Hollywood movies on the mobile phone does not seem to be what people are willing to pay for (45%). (Hutchison 3G Austria, 2003)

This might be slightly surprising for mobile operators since most of these services are also possible using existing 2G network infrastructure. When evaluating whether to invest in 3G or not, mobile service providers focused on technical solutions to deliver broadband content to mobile devices. When landline broadband internet became available, experts saw the "destiny of the Internet […] to transmit Hollywood movies into our homes" (Thackara, 2001, p. 48). Consequently, mobile service providers expected a huge demand for small video clips or even complete Hollywood movies on small screens of cellphones as well. Many of their cost estimations were based on large data transfer volumes. That is why the key to success of 3G technologies like UMTS will be applications with bandwidth requirements at the upper end of the available range and those which use the new technologies that are offered by 3G. (König, 2001) Figure 1 shows the different services that were available in different network generations in a roadmap.

Electromagnetic radiation of cellphones and transmitters has been an issue of controversial discussion in the past. On the one hand, customers expect high voice quality and large area coverage but on the other hand, they fear the radiation of electronic devices. In Germany, four 2G service providers set up about 50,000 transmitter stations, another 40,000 will be required for the 3G migration. However, 3G uses another technology which minimizes the impacts of mobile communication, both when establishing a connection and during the call.[2] (Gneiting & Demmelhuber, 2002)

3.2. Organizational and Technological Requirements of 3G Systems

To offer new 3G services, a new network had to be implemented that added another layer to the existing 2G networks. This was done as a fallback to 2G services wherever 3G coverage was not available. The basic framework for 3G services has been defined in the International Mobile Telecommunications at 2000 MHz (=IMT-2000) standard by the International Telecommunication Union (=ITU). Since there had been difficulties with many different frequencies used in 2G and different multiplexing methods, the aim was to completely standardize 3G services. (Schreiber, 2002, p. 79-111) However, this proved to be difficult as some frequencies were still occupied for other purposes (see Figure 2), especially in the USA.

In addition to that, three different 'types' of 3G evolved:

---

[2] Further reading about electromagnetic radiation: Gneiting, S. & Demmelhuber, S. (2002). Strahleninferno oder Öko-Funk? UMTS und die Strahlendebatte. c't. (CD-ROM).

- In Europe, Wideband Code Division Multiple Access (=W-CDMA) has been chosen as the evolution path from GSM to 3G services and adds another layer using Frequency Division Duplex (=FDD) and Time Division Duplex (=TDD) multiplexing techniques. W-CDMA based 3G networks are marketed under the brand name UMTS.
- In Asian countries, Time Division Code Division Multiple Access (=TD-CDMA) has been favored to be used in 3G systems using only TDD multiplexing techniques in a narrowband CDMA environment (called Universal Wireless Consortium UWC-136).
- In the USA and other countries that formerly used CDMA-based 2G services, Code Division Multiple Access – Revision 2000 (=CDMA2000) has been chosen as the new air interface instead of W-CDMA because it can co-exist with existing systems using FDD and TDD multiplexing techniques as well. (Nicopolitidis, Papadimitriou, Obaidat & Pomportsis, 2003)

Nevertheless, about 90% of the 110 operators having granted a 3G license until August 2002 decided on W-CDMA technology for their core networks. (UMTS-Forum, 2002)

In addition to different technologies, cell site sizes in 3G environments differ from 2G networks. 3G uses four types of cell site covering areas of different sizes:

- *Pico-Cells* have a radius of only some 10 meters, but offer a data transfer speed of up to 2 Megabit per second (=Mbps) at low mobility like at hot spots
- *Micro-Cells* have a radius of some 100 meters. They offer data transfer speeds of up to 2 Mbps at hot spots or within business districts in large cities
- *Macro-Cells* have a radius of approximately 5-20 kilometers. Data transfer speeds are up to 384 Kilobit per second (=kbps) which is also available at high traveling speeds.
- *World-Cells, Umbrella-Cells or Hyper-Cells* have a radius of up to several hundred kilometers, but only offer relatively slow data transfer speeds.

In the GSM world, sizes of cell sites differ between 900 MHz (GSM-900) based networks and those using a frequency of 1800 MHz (DCS-1800). GSM-900 cells have a radius of 35 to 100 kilometers whereas DCS-1800 cells can only cover an area having a radius of 8 kilometers. (Wang, 2003; Teltarif, n.d. b) Consequently, a large number of new cell-sites have to be set up to offer 3G services which cause high costs for mobile service operators, in addition to technological challenges of the new system.

3.3. Billions for Fresh Air – Licensing of Frequencies

To start 3G services, mobile operators had to get permission to use the respective frequencies in countries all over the world. In most of the countries, there were more applicants than available licenses. To cope with that, some countries started a 'beauty-contest' but most of them auctioned the licenses. In Germany, licenses were auctioned in August 2000 to six (T-Mobil, Vodafone, E-Plus, O2, Quam and Mobilcom) auctioneers for almost 50 billion Euro, whereof the first four companies had an existing 2G network running in Germany.[3] (BWCS, 2003) Having paid about 8 billion Euro, mobile operators in Germany found themselves in a difficult economic situation and the auctioning system and the requirement to cover a certain amount of the German population at a given date was heavily criticized. To avoid that in future, licenses for upcoming wireless technologies will be sold at 'administration costs' in all European countries. (Jaeger, 2002) However, the president of the 'Regulierungsbehörde für Telekommunikation und Post' that hosted the auction in Germany seems convinced that in the long run UMTS pays off for the companies. (König, 2002)

3.4. Implementation and Roll-Out of 3G Systems

The first commercial 3G network was launched in Japan by NTT DoCoMo in October 2001. At first, there was a run on 3G handsets, but sales dropped soon after the launch. (Teltarif, n. d. a) One of the reasons for such a slow start was the lack of sophisticated mobile phones, especially for those that supported a hand over between existing area-wide 2G networks and areas with 3G coverage. (Kuri, 2003) This might also be a reason, why the globally operating mobile service provider Hutchison only attracted about 520,000 customers in its five active 3G networks (Italy, UK, Australia, Sweden, Austria) until mid of 2003. At first, Hutchison estimated one million customers just in the UK until end of 2003, but now the company forecasts the same target for all their existing networks together. (Sokolov, 2003)

Another reason why consumers still await further development is because many services that were promised by 3G have become available in existing 2G networks with only minor upgrades. The impacts of this issue will be discussed in chapter 5.1.

3.5. Comparison between User Expectations and the actual Experience

By now, UMTS and the other 3G technologies turned out to be very disappointing to customers. Even in Japan, where people are supposed to adopt new technologies very quickly, sale forecasts had to be lowered from 1.38 million to 0.32 million sold handsets in the financial year 2002/2003 by NTT DoCoMo even though the company continu-

---

[3] Further reading about 3G licensing worldwide: BWCS (Pub.). (2003). *3G Status Report*. Retrieved September 08, 2003, from http://www.bwcs.com/free_reports/BWCS_3G.pdf.

ously increased the network's coverage. (Winter, 2002) In addition to that, 3G mobile phones are much more difficult to produce and therefore more expensive. A study found out that a 2G phone consists in the average of 331 components and costs about 56 US$ to produce whereas two sample 3G cell phones that were available at this time consisted of 544 / 702 components and cost 127 / 280 US$ to produce. (Globisch & Winter, 2002) Moreover, the maximum data transfer rate of 2 Mbps which was promised by 3G will only be available around so-called hot spots at slow pace, so mobile high speed access in trains or cars impossible, at least in the early stages of the 3G era. There is also competition not from the telecommunication industry, but from the computing sector. Wireless LAN (=WLAN) is a new and emerging technology that offers data transfer speeds of up to 54 Mbps at hot spots but uses a frequency which is not regulated by governments and can be used free of charge. A researcher of McKinsey estimated that the price for one megabyte data transfer at a hot spot will cost about 20 to 25 Euro-Cent using UMTS whereas costs are as low as 3 to 6 Euro-Cent when using WLAN instead. (Sietmann, 2001)

In Germany, there is no date announced when UMTS is to be launched. Quam and Mobilcom that obtained a 3G license have already stopped their 3G business because of financial difficulties. So, only the four existing 2G providers are still working on their 3G networks which will probably be launched some time in 2004. (Dernbach, 2003)

4. Fourth Generation – The Future of Mobile Communications

4.1. How to define 4G?

Yet, there is no common definition of what 4G entails. Most of the sources found state that a further increase in bandwidth and a combination of different technologies are the issues that characterize the 4G technology which is supposed to be available at the end of the decade. Perera (2001, p. 76) stated that the term 4G "could encourage users to defer trying out 3G in the belief that something more advanced is around the corner". Since the rollout of 3G in many countries, especially in Europe, is delayed, the question arises, which specific new services are available using 4G and when it will become available to the public. The first question is difficult to answer, because there is still no consensus. However, 4G will not be a family of technologies like those being defined in IMT-2000, but integrates about 20 different technologies together allowing handover and roaming in different network architectures or platforms. In addition to that, there will not only be cell phones or personal digital assistants (=PDA) to be used in wireless environments, but also TVs, DVD players or even fridges – "just about anything you can conceivably put a transceiver in and assign an IP address to" (Tanner, 2003, p. 20) can be used making 4G use ubiquitous. The question of when 4G will be available is being discussed in chapters 4.3 and 4.4

4.2. The Idea behind 4G

Critics state, that 4G is eventually supposed to offer what people were promised by 3G: a high-speed globally accepted radio transmission standard developed for data transmission by numerous different devices. By using three different technologies (see chapter 3.2) for 3G, all standardization efforts failed. (Computer Business Review, 2001) Therefore, 4G is designed to be completely different from traditional voice-oriented networks but "represents purely packet/IP-based cellular wireless that pushes switching intelligence away from the network core". (Swasey, 2002, p. 12) Therefore, a 4G network has to be implemented as a decentralized system with end-to-end IP-services, not only in the air interface, but also in the core network. Researchers aim at data transfer speeds of up to 100 Mbps and latencies similar to those of wired networks. Intelligent networks not using centralized circuit switching any more do need sophisticated devices with more processing power. Nevertheless, in the end prices per bit are supposed to be lower compared to 3G. (Swasey, 2002)

The most important improvement of 4G is that it allows "global roaming across multiple wireless and mobile networks [...] [so] users will have access to different services, increased coverage, the convenience of a single device, one bill with reduced total access cost, and more reliable wireless access even with the failure or loss of one or more networks". (Varshney & Jain, 2001, p. 94) Multimode devices have to be developed containing numerous interfaces to communicate in heterogeneous network environments. In addition to that, horizontal (between transmitters within the same network type) and vertical (between different layers of the network) handover has to be supported to guarantee worldwide coverage both at highest speeds and lowest costs. (Varshney & Jain, 2001) For the air interface, a combination of Variable Spreading Factor Orthogonal Frequency and Code Division Multiplexing (=VSF-OFCDM) for downstream traffic and Variable Spreading Factor Code Division Multiple Access (=VSF-CDMA) for upstream traffic will be employed that offers high speeds and superior reliability, even in adverse conditions. (Zivadinovic, 2003) Even though the standards are not approved by the ITU yet, Japanese companies financially supported by the Japanese government are working on basic specifications that might be the basis for the final standard to be approved by the ITU which will probably take place in 2007. (Network Briefing Daily, 2001a; Grayson, 2003)

4.3. Credibility of Mobile Provider's Promises

In chapter 3.5, it was discovered that user expectations and provider promises in regard to 3G differ. Sales lagged behind forecasts due to the unavailability of sophisticated handsets and new applications that made use of the new technology. People were not willing to pay money for new services or technology that did not add value to their life. Consequently, the question arose whether real customer demand was considered and evaluated properly. (Thackara, 2001) In addition to that, the launch of 3G networks was repeatedly delayed by mobile operators, especially in Europe. Many people might have lost confidence in their promises, not only in regard to the availability but also in regard to the capabilities of the new technology. Therefore, operators have to be careful not to sap customers confidence when implementing 3G because it might even influence the success of forthcoming generations. In 2001, industry experts and NTT DoCoMo predicted a commercial start of 4G in 2006/2007 which was about four years prior to the expected launch when research in 4G was started. (Network Briefing Daily, 2001b) However, the ITU "quietly decided end of last year to delay the rollout of fourth-generation mobile-phone systems by five years" (Jeffrey, 2003, p. 4) from 2010/2015 to 2015/2020 which was primarily driven by European Telecommunication companies which felt that "it's not the time to start that now" (Jeffrey, 2003, p. 4). The real reason for that might be high sunk costs for 3G licenses and huge investments in the respective network infrastructure. In addition to that, there seem to be technical difficulties in regard to background noise, wave reflections from obstacles or even changes in their air temperature that affect the wireless data transmission process. Besides technical and financial issues, the choice of a frequency for the use of 4G is another problem to be addressed. In 2007, the ITU will finally decide whether to use the 5 GHz band or another one. (Grayson, 2003) Until then, research and development of network infrastructure incurs a risk which might delay the entire implementation process again.

4G could have been the first mobile technology to arrive earlier than expected, but detention and dissention might prove once again the doubtfulness of operator promises.

4.4. Current State of 4G Technology Research

Research on 4G technology was primarily conducted in Asia, particularly in South Korea and Japan, where governments spent large amounts of money to support companies working on 4G development. (Network Briefing Daily, 2001b; Multimedia Futures, 2001) NTT DoCoMo is an early adopter of new technologies which is reflected by the set up of the first commercial 3G network worldwide in 2001 and in research of follow-up technologies now known as 4G which was started in 1998. Therefore, an indoor demo site had been set up in March 2002 consisting of only one base station and one mobile station. (Schäfer, 2002) The test environment fulfilled NTT DoCoMo's expectations offering a data transfer rate from the base station to the mobile station of 100 Mbps downstream and upstream speeds of up to 20 Mbps occupying a bandwidth of about 100 MHz. (RCR Wireless News, 2002) Driven by this success, NTT DoCoMo applied at the local government for a license to do a field test in Yokosuka, Japan. Permission was granted end of May 2003. Even though NTT DoCoMo's aim was to employ 4G technology in 2006 already, the company now tries to officially launch 4G services around the year 2010. (Kyodo News International, 2003)

5. The x.5 Generations – Technological Milestones or Human Failure at Technological Challenges

5.1. 2.5G – The next step towards Delivery of Multimedia Content to Handheld Devices or just "UMTS-light"?

Like any new technology the 2G network standards were under continuous review and improvement from the beginning on. The initial definition of the European GSM standard (called 'Phase 1') in 1991 was designed to allow voice and some simple 'additional services' such as call forwarding to a mailbox or blocking of incoming or outgoing calls. The main focus was on compatibility with existing analogue and digital wired networks. In 'Phase 2', which was adopted in 1994, first connection-based simple data transmissions and additional services that were common for wired digital networks like the transmission of the caller's telephone number became available. The next revision of the GSM standard called 'Phase 2+"was finalized in 1996. It allows for the specialties of data communication in comparison to voice communication. In former connection-based networks, a full voice channel had to be reserved for data transmissions even though data throughput varied over time which caused inefficiencies and high costs because customers had to pay for the time they were connected. The new approach of 'Phase 2+' was to use a packet-oriented transmission or to combine several channels either to improve performance or to cut costs. (Duque-Antón, 2002, p. 63-74)

HSCSD (1996) used new error correcting mechanisms and combined several channels simultaneously which resulted in data transfer speeds of 14.4 kbps per channel. The maximum data transfer speed was 56.7 kbps by using four channels. Many network resources were occupied since HSCSD was still circuit-switched and users were charged for every single channel they used. Consequently, HSCSD was not accepted by customers. (Duque-Antón, 2002, p. 185-186)

GPRS (1998) was completely packet-oriented allowing variable data transfer rates of up to 171.2kbps in GSM networks. To achieve this speed, eight time slots with a transfer speed of 21.4 kbps each had to be combined. Initially, UMTS was invented as a stopgap until UMTS became available. Since a date for the adoption of UMTS in Germany is still uncertain, GPRS became more and more popular because it allowed UMTS-like services in existing 2G network infrastructure. (Duque-Antón, 2002, p. 186-187)

Since many multimedia services like picture messaging, polyphonic ringtones, instant messaging, email and web browsing are already available using GPRS, it seems to be unlikely that people are willing to pay more money for the same services but use another way of accessing them. Surprisingly, SMS have become the killer application of 2G, but currently there is no killer application known that uses the full capabilities of UMTS. (König, 2001) It might be regarded as an act of desperation that mobile operators and German ministries have opened up a website[4] with a competition asking customers to invent innovative services and applications that might become killer applications in 3G.

The adoption of UMTS is supposed to be slow in the early years. Less than 30% of all mobile subscribers worldwide will use the new technology by the year 2010 according to market studies by the UMTS-Forum (2002). If only a few people use the system from the beginning on, it might be doubtful whether mobile operators continue to add 3G coverage in rural areas. In Germany, operators are forced to provide coverage to a certain percentage of the population at given dates. However, there might not be many incentives to offer high speeds of up to 2 Mbps in rural areas except for some hot spots. But at hot spots, wireless internet access could be provided at much lower costs using WLAN casting the success of UMTS into doubt. (Sietmann, 2001)

Furthermore, there is another technology called Enhanced Data rates for Global Evolution (=EDGE) that combines the advantages of HSCSD and GPRS. It easily integrates

---

[4] Ideenwettbewerb UMTS Rheinland-Pfalz, URL: http://ideenwettbewerb-umts.rlp.de

into existing 2G networks but offers data transfer speeds of up to 384 kbps, which will be similar to speeds that are offered by UMTS in the beginning. EDGE was originally developed to offer a high speed alternative to UMTS for mobile operators that did not get a frequency license. Consequently, it has to be located somewhere in between 2.5G and 3G. In Germany, all four major mobile service providers obtained a license, so they do not have any incentives to implement EDGE in their networks. (Duque-Antón, 2002, p. 187-188)

5.2. 3.5G – Is an improved Version of 3G necessary to offer Features that we were promised by UMTS itself?

So far, 3G has had a difficult start. It seems that mobile broadband internet access at 2 Mbps which customers were promised will remain a great dream, at least beyond the range of hot spots. Even though operators will never admit that current 3G implementations might not meet their expectations, they are working on modifications to improve the performance. By the end of 2003, '3G Release D' supporting download speeds of up to 3.1 Mbps will be released. (Schwartz, 2003) However, the newest improvement to 3G called High Speed Downlink Packet Access (=HSDPA) will only work in conjunction with W-CDMA. Consequently, the ITU asked carriers using narrowband CDMA to switch to W-CDMA. But due a limited range of frequencies that are available in the USA, operators do not have the possibility to do that. (Dornan, 2002)

A large variety of different incompatible standards can be a restraint in the roll out of 3G and make upgrade paths to upcoming generations a challenge. The initial aim of 3G was to provide a worldwide standard for ubiquitous mobile broadband internet access in a network that was especially designed for data communications. Thinking about upgrades for a network that hardly exists does not show confidence of network operators and reveals weaknesses in the development and evaluation process of the new technology. 3.5 will just be another patchwork trying to fix a poorly conceived system. Driven by such a pessimistic future, critics state that one will primarily remember UMTS in Europe because it precipitated the break down of the European mobile service industry. (Kuri, 2001)

6. Using Seven League Boots to jump from 2.5G to 4G?

Keeping all technical difficulties and the financial burden in mind that mobile operators have to cope with during the roll-out of 3G the question arises whether it might be favorable from a technological and financial perspective to skip one generation and jump directly from existing 2.5G to 4G. In the course of this paper it appeared that issues like network decentralization and data oriented network architectures that were envisaged by 3G finally did not turn out in a satisfying way. Continuous delays in the set up of the 3G infrastructure left a performance gap that could be filled by employing WLAN technology at hot spots as a "stepping stone to 4G as it introduces the concept of pervasive wireless broadband connectivity anytime, anywhere". (Lee, 2003) Facing these problems, some providers already wrote down their investments in 3G licenses or even thought about withdrawing from 3G markets in favor of 4G which seems to have a sound business case. (Economist, 2003) Others state that 3G was ahead of the times when it was announced by mobile operators like other technologies such as Asynchronous Transfer Mode (=ATM) or WAP which finally failed. (Electronics Weekly, 2002a) In about five years time, as a mature technology, it might be successful replacing 2G that was "perhaps the most successful electronic product of all time. […] But by then it will probably be called 4G anyway." (Electronics Weekly, 2002b)

From a consumer perspective, there does not seem to be high demand for 3G because alternative technologies can offer similar benefits at lower costs. Consumers do not want to buy a certain technology, but services that add value to their life. This is also an explanation why KDDI, Japans second largest mobile operator, was more successful than the first mover NTT DoCoMo in attracting customers for their new services and applications. "Disillusioned with the 3G jargon and skeptical of its abilities", people preferred KDDI's network whose marketing campaign focused on easiness of use, competitive pricing and useful services instead of technology. Basically it was not even called 3G technology. (Strategic Direction, 2003)

This also explains the phenomenon that already appeared when the two services called TS21 and TS22 were adopted in GSM Phase 2+. Nobody would have cared about these two services is they were marketed in a technical way. But they promoted as a service that enabled people to send SMS from their cell phones which was an added value. So customers were willing to pay for it. (Duque-Antón, 2002, p. 70-71). Since the discussion about 3G already left a bittersweet feeling in people's mind, mobile operators should really consider the alternative of skipping 3G in favor of 2.5G and WLAN until 4G systems will be available.

7. Conclusion
In the course of the investigation, the evolution process from analogue mobile commu-

nications to digital broadband mobile coverage has been outlined. 2G systems that are still predominant in the world gained a huge subscriber base. Currently, the telecommunications industry is at the crossroads. Having paid billions of dollars for frequency licenses required to offer 3G services, many operators now struggle in developing new applications and setting up their network. In countries where 3G is already up and running, sales lag behind forecast and services prove to be disappointing. There are various reasons for this unsatisfying situation, both for the customers and for mobile operators. Apparently, 2.5G can offer similar performance to 3G but uses existing infrastructure with only minor modifications. High speed data transmissions that were promised by 3G will only take place at hot spots, but WLAN as a competing technology can be employed at much lower costs. So the question remains where 3G can be deployed. Standardization efforts in regard to frequency use and multiplexing techniques that were another aim of 3G also failed. By patching 3G to 3.5, the problem will not be solved but made worse.

When designing 4G, it was focused on the integration of many different wireless standards in an end-to-end IP-based network offering unprecedented data transfer speeds at lower costs than 3G. Consequently, mobile operators might consider skipping one generation. Customers that were promised high speed internet access b 3G are getting disappointed of continuous delays and lose confidence in operator's promises. Moreover, operators have to recoup costs of frequency licenses and 3G infrastructure. Costs will have to be passed on to the customers. But customers do not care about technical details and technologies. They do not want to pay for 3G if they can use similar services at lower costs using another technology like GPRS. The overall 3G situation might be different, at least in Germany, if one established 2G operator had not received a 3G license because EDGE would have been implemented allowing customers to use multimedia content on their cell phone. Since this did not happen, people in Germany and many other countries still have to wait for 3G. But perhaps, there will be a provider that skips 3G and jumps directly to 4G providing GPRS or EDGE-based services in the meantime. 4G is not far away. It is almost there and could be one out of a few technologies that arrives on time or even earlier if 3G operators do no longer delay the standardization process fearing losses in their 3G business. This seems so true against the background of the futurologist Alvin Toffler's statement in the Economist (2003, p. 61): "The future always comes too fast, and in the wrong order."

Index of Appendices

Appendix

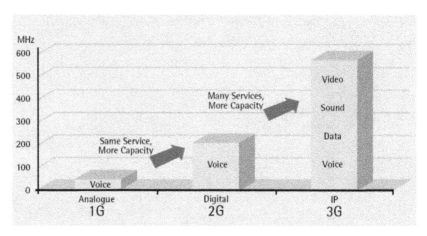

Figure 1 The case for more spectrum

Source: UMTS-Forum (Pub.). (2002). *Evolution to 3G/UMTS services*. Retrieved September 15, 2003, from http://www.3gnewsroom.com/html/whitepapers/2002/WHITE_PAPER_1.zip. p. 4.

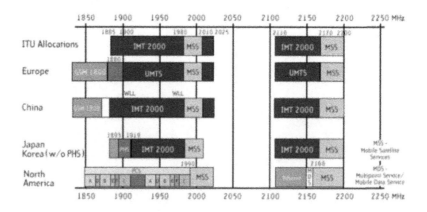

Figure 2 Frequencies used by mobile technologies

Source: *Cellular News*, Retrieved September 30, 2003, from http://www.cellular-news.com/images/3g_spectrum.gif.

References

Books

Duque-Antón, M. (2002). *Mobilfunknetze – Grundlagen, Dienste und Protokolle.* Braunschweig: Vieweg.

Lescuyer, P. (2002). *UMTS – Grundlagen, Architektur und Standard.* Heidelberg: dpunkt-Verlag.

Schreiber, G. A. (2002). *UMTS – Märkte, Potenziale, Geschäftsmodelle.* Köln: Deutscher Wirtschaftsdienst.

Walke, B. (2001). *Mobilfunknetze und ihre Protokolle 1 – Grundlagen, GSM, UMTS und andere zellulare Mobilfunknetze* (3rd ed.). Stuttgart: Teubner.

Journals, Magazines, Conference Papers and Online Sources

BWCS (Pub.). (2003). *3G Status Report.* Retrieved September 08, 2003, from http://www.bwcs.com/free_reports/BWCS_3G.pdf.

Cellular Online (Pub.). (2003). *Latest global, handset, base station, & regional cellular statistics.* Retrieved September 19, 2003, from http://www.cellular.co.za/stats/stats-main.htm.

Computer Business Review (Pub.). (2001). The 4G bandwagon starts to roll. 9(3). p. 44.

Dornan, A. (2002). Fast forward to 4G? *Network Magazine.* 17(3). p. 34-39.

Electronics Weekly (Pub.). (2002a). Talking about 3G does not make it any more 'real'. (2044). p. 20.

Electronics Weekly (Pub.). (2002b). Talk of 4G is no panacea to the ills of the 3G roll-out. (2076). p. 20.

Hutchison 3G Austria (Pub.). (2003). *3G Markt: Prognosen und Märkte*. Retrieved September 20, 2003, from http://www.drei.at/SelectMenu.wa?seIDM=189AE02D-1C39-46BA-9DAA-2DF8170190CD.

Jeffrey, S. (2003). 4G (yes, 4G) delayed. *RCR Wireless News*. 22(3). p. 4.

Koljonen, T. (2001). *Mobile system technologies beyond current 3G*. Proceedings of the 2001 symposium on applications and internet-workshops. IEEE.

König, W. (2001). Wege aus dem UMTS-Dilemma gesucht. *Wirtschaftsinformatik* 43(3). p. 221-222.

König, W. (2002). Interview mit dem Präsidenten der Regulierungsbehörde für Telekommunikation und Post Matthias Kurth. *Wirtschaftsinformatik*. 44(6). p. 591-597.

Multimedia Futures (Pub.). (2001). Japan sets sights on 4G already. (272). p. 6.

Nicopolitidis, P., Papadimitriou, G. I., Obaidat, M. S. & Pomportsis, A. S. (2003). Third Generation and beyond wireless systems. *Communications of the ACM*. 46(8). p. 120-124.

Perera, R. (2001). Researchers outline vision of next-generation 4G wireless. *InfoWorld*. 23(13). p. 76B-76D.

RCR Wireless News (Pub.). (2002). DoCoMo says 4G transmission test successful. 21(41). p. 35.

Schwartz, E. (2003). 4G takes to the air. *InfoWorld*. 25(24). p. 14-15.

Strategic Direction (Pub.). (2003). 3G strategy at Nokia, NTT DoCoMo and AT&T. 19(1). p. 13-16.

Swasey, L. (2002). Time for 4G? *Telecommunications – American Edition*. 36(14). p. 12.

Tanner, J. C. (2003). 4G – The silent revolution. *Wireless Asia*. 6(2). p. 20-21.

Thackara, J. (2001). The design challenge of pervasive computing. *interactions*. 8(3). p. 46-52.

UMTS-Forum (Pub.). (2002). *Evolution to 3G/UMTS services*. Retrieved September 15, 2003, from http://www.3gnewsroom.com/html/whitepapers/2002/WHITE_PAPER_1.zip.

Varshney, U. & Jain, R. (2001). Issues in emerging 4G wireless networks. *Communications*. 34(6).

Wang, B. H. (2003). *Cellular mobile radio*. Retrieved September 29, 2003, from http://santos.ee.ntu.edu.tw/~mobcom/Download/Cellualr%20Concept.pdf.

Newspapers

Economist (Pub.). (2003). Move over 3G – Here comes 4G. 367(8326). p. 61-62.

Kyodo News International (Pub.). (2003). NTT DoCoMo to test 4G mobile communications system. (May 28, 2003).

Lee, C. (2003). Wireless LAN – A stepping stone to 4G? *New Straits Times – Management Times*. (March 05, 2003).

Grayson, I. (2003). Long haul across the generation gap – Special report. *The Australian*. (July 22, 2003).

Network Briefing Daily (Pub.). (2001a). Japan finalizes basic specs for 4G. (November 05, 2001).

Network Briefing Daily (Pub.). (2001b). South Korea prepares early start to 4G development. (November 09, 2001).

Slodczyk, K. (2003). Mobiles Internet – Teurer Schnickschnack. *Handelsblatt*. (August 25, 2003).

Offline-Databases

Gneiting, S. & Demmelhuber, S. (2002). Strahleninferno oder Öko-Funk? UMTS und die Strahlendebatte. *c't*. (CD-ROM).

Jaeger, S. (2002). EU will Funkfrequenz-Vergabepraxis ändern. *c't*. (CD-ROM).

Sietmann, R. (2001). WLAN versus UMTS – Anwendungsentwickler zweifeln an UMTS-Erfolg. *c't*. (CD-ROM).

Online-News Channels

Dernbach, C. (2003). *UMTS-Start in Deutschland nicht in Sicht*. Retrieved September 23, 2003, from http://www.heise.de/newsticker/data/jk-02.09.03-006/.

Globisch, J. & Winter, M.-A. (2002). *Eckdaten von 3G-Handys im Vergleich zu 2G-Handys*. Retrieved September 21, 2003, from http://www.teltarif.de/arch/2002/kw40/s8967.html.

Kuri, J. (2001). *Nebenbuhler und Nachfolger von UMTS*. Retrieved September 26, 2003, from http://www.heise.de/bin/nt.print/newsticker/data/jk-25.02.01-004/?id=b1eb3614&todo=print.

Kuri, J. (2003). *Nokia beginnt mit Auslieferung von UMTS Handys*. Retrieved September 04, 2003, from http://www.heise.de/bin/nt.print/newsticker/data/jk-13.06.03-003/?id=c86f490d&todo=print.

Schäfer, V. (2002). *NTT DoCoMo experimentiert mit 4G*. Retrieved September 26, 2003, from http://www.teltarif.de/arch/2002/kw12/s7534.html.

Sokolov, D. (2003). *Hutchison hat bislang weltweit 520.000 UMTS-Kunden [Update]*. Retrieved September 06, 2003, from http://www.heise.de/bin/nt.print/newsticker/data/jk-21.08.03-010/?id=bf12f648&todo=print.

Teltarif (Pub.). (n.d. a). *UMTS – Technik, Chancen, Utopien.* Retrieved September 27, 2003, from http://www.teltarif.de/i/umts.html.

Teltarif (Pub.). (n.d. b). *UMTS und GSM – ein Vergleich.* Retrieved September 27, 2003, from http://www.teltarif.de/i/umts-technik.html.

Winter, M.-A. (2002). *UMTS-Handys verkaufen sich schlecht.* Retrieved September 21, 2003, from http://www.teltarif.de/arch/2002/kw45/s9216.html.

Zivadinovic, D. (2003). *Japanisches Pilotprojekt für Mobilfunksystem der vierten Generation.* Retrieved September 20, 2003, from http://www.heise.de/bin/nt.print/newsticker/data/dz-31.05.03-001/?id=f389207e&todo=print.